SPINNING

SPINNING

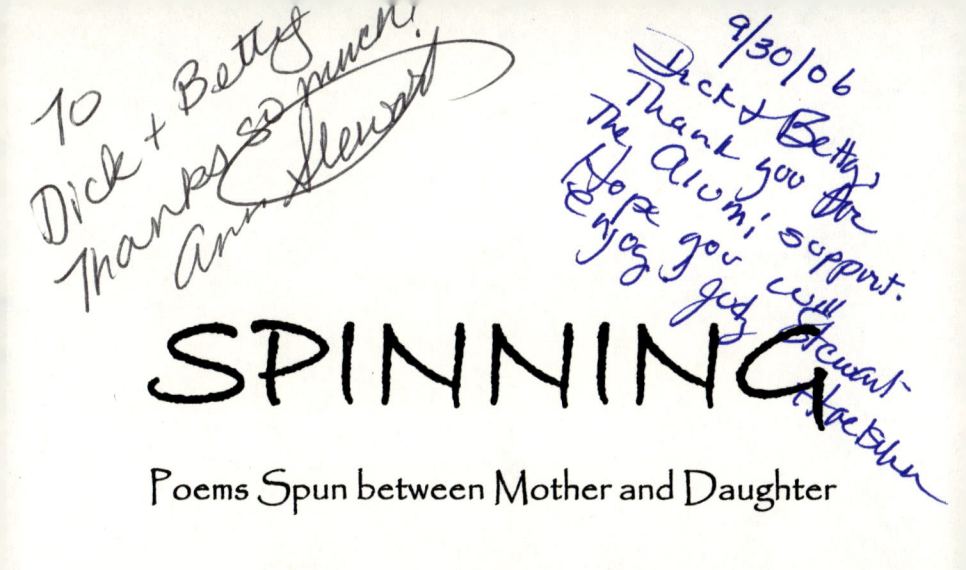

Poems Spun between Mother and Daughter

by Ann Stewart
with Judy Stewart Hoelscher

Introductory haiku by Barb Groh

Alumni Association of Bronson Methodist Hospital
School of Nursing
2006

© 2006
Alumni Association of Bronson Methodist Hospital
School of Nursing

All rights reserved.

Stewart, Ann, 1975–
    Spinning: Poems spun between mother and daughter, by Ann Stewart with Judy Stewart Hoelscher. Introductory haiku, by Barb Groh. Kalamazoo, Mich.: Alumni Association of Bronson Methodist Hospital School of Nursing, 2006.
    x,134 p.

    1. Mothers and daughters—Poetry 2. Poetry—Therapeutic use 3. Rheumatoid arthritis in0020children I. Title II. Hoelscher, Judy Stewart, 1943– III. Groh, Barbara, 1945–
PS327 S849   811.08 S849

ISBN: 0-9763413-3-6

Contents

Introduction	1
I. Infection	17
II. Rehabilitation	51
III. Recovery	95
Acknowledgements	129
Resources	131
About the Authors	133

Spinning

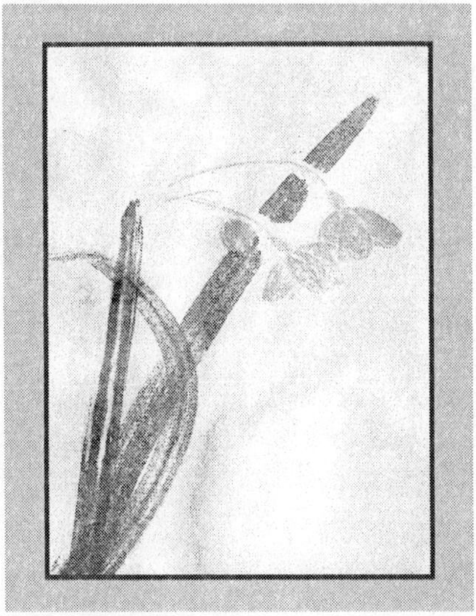

Spinning

Introduction

Spinning...
Mother. Daughter.
Tales—traumas, trivia, triumphs
told, twirled, threaded

to tapestry—Woven lives.
Choices. Chances taken.
Meanings...

Memories hidden in fabric's
Folds until freed and given voice.
Daughter. Mother.
Spinning...

— *B. Groh, 2006*

Spinning

Wendell Berry said it well.

> "Within the circles of our lives
> we dance the circles of the years,
> the circles of the season
> within the circles of years.
>
> Again again we come and go
> Changed, changing. Hands
> Join, unjoin in love and fear,
> Grief and joy. The circles turn,
> Each giving into each, into all
> Only music keeps us here,
> Each by all the other held."

The story of a mother and daughter does that as their lives cycle and each learns from the other. Hearts crossed in living the life they make and that is given to them. Loving and sharing to make it through.

Introduction

Let Me Introduce You to Annie. 1983

She is six years old, has brown hair and eyes, and is of average weight but short for her age. She likes dolls, drawing, Little Thinker Tapes, dressing up and lots of very normal activities that most six-year-olds enjoy. Annie has juvenile rheumatoid arthritis (JRA) and has been diagnosed for one year, although symptoms were present before that time. A closer look at Annie reveals large, puffy, knobby knees, puffy ankles and large middle joints on fingers and toes; all are joints that contribute to a very stiff walk, awkward running form and inability to jump more than six inches without experiencing pain.

The fact that she has JRA is not greatly significant to Annie. Her life proceeds very normally. She continues to enjoy her family, the people she interacts with, both in the health care system and in the family's circle of acquaintance. She adjusts to all pain and altered activity with one exception, and that is her fear of needles and having blood drawn. The pain that she has experienced and continues to experience has altered her behavior somewhat as she often has not been her smiling, amiable self—whining and crying more readily than would be warranted in a normal situation.

Spinning

The onset of Annie's JRA is significant as it was typical of many and may provide insight for both parents and members of the health care team that are concerned with assessing the health care status of children. She had for at least one year prior to her June 1980 diagnosis a large, swollen middle finger joint that was neither red nor painful. It was watched closely, and the assumption was made that it was the result of trauma and would return to normal. Instead, the finger increased in size until it was one and one half times normal. She complained intermittently of aching knees and neck, pain that responded to one dose of aspirin, and normal activity would be resumed after a night's rest. "Growing pains," everyone said. She gradually became more sedentary as she spent hours listening to tapes, reading books and drawing. While others ran and played, Annie sat or lay and listened or colored.

In February 1980, the family went to Disneyland, Florida, and on a cold, snowy, windy day, rode the rides and saw the sights. Annie complained of pain in her knees and limped that morning. She cried off and on throughout the day but was impatiently encouraged to walk. She was frightened of a number of the sights and upset throughout the day. Malingering was suspected by Mother, a strange

Introduction

response from a mother who knows enough about human growth and development and her daughter to know that this behavior was grossly abnormal.

My response was related to having just returned from California and a visit with a father who had a very sudden and unexpected major heart attack. I was not open to seeing any more illness - did not want it to be. In the following days Annie refused (intermittently) to walk in the morning and was carried to the bathroom or to the pool. During this period, of time she limped markedly but would never admit to feeling pain. On returning home, the symptoms subsided although an appointment was made to see the family physician who said to watch the symptoms and call him when they were acute.

Another call from California came to say that Grandmother was to have a G. I. malignancy removed on the following day. Attention switched to both Grandfather and Grandmother, and Annie's symptoms were not attended to until after Grandpa and Grandma's two major surgeries and life had settled somewhat. By June 1980, Annie had a large middle toe and a puzzling lump on her left wrist along with previously described pain in her knees, ankles, and toes. The persistent pain and altered gait caused

Spinning

a great concern, and my nursing colleagues were consulted regarding the symptoms—still "wishing" them to go away—and they did not.

The diagnosis (99% sure) was made after a visit to the pediatrician who explained the three types of JRA briefly and shared his feeling that Annie was of the type that would outgrow the disease in adolescence. But that did not happen and she has had it, will have it, for life.

The pain and sadness I felt (as Annie's mother) at this time are hard to describe, and yet I will attempt to do so because I believe that persons involved in the health care system are not aware or forget what is happening to persons in this or like situations. The behavior that parents use is directly related to the feelings they are experiencing and their individual coping mechanisms. Success in promoting health with families who have a child with JRA may be directly related to being able to understand and deal with behaviors used. Although some of my feelings were related to the combination of sudden illness in our family, I am aware that most other parents experience like feelings also, as I have had the opportunity to share my feelings and discuss this aspect with other parents in our local JRA parents group. A part of the feeling has to do with the guilt associated with the lengthy pre-diagnosis time that could have been averted and therapy started earlier in the onset of the disease thus avoiding progression of the symptoms. A large part of the feeling has to do with the normal parental concern for one's children's well being and ability to experience a normal, happy life. Our culture emphasizes the beautiful body and active pursual of life. I want Annie to have that chance, and the threat that JRA makes to that is frightening.

— *J. Stewart Hoelscher*

The Cycle: A Darker Connotation. 2006

The struggle of modern women, to me, is reminiscent of a cycle of health—which probably shouldn't be a cycle at all. (One gets sick, one takes cure, one is better, right?) Our independence has come with a price, so we feel self-doubt and regret for being independent (rather than demanding respect for opting to pay that price, as men would). We also realize that once having had our freedom, we cannot live without it.

As one of many pioneering women determined to seek their own careers and be free of traditional roles, my mother fought the forces of guilt over and over. Swimming against a current of adversity, self-doubt was always a major obstacle. Have I caused my daughter's illness by not being home? Do I cast off my early marriage and follow my feelings? What punishment comes next for choosing my own way? How do I return to embrace my independence when it has seemed to be a source of so much harm?

I, on the other hand, have joined a society in which women are expected to be perfect wives and diligent mothers AND have success at a career. We are constantly determined to be as independent as men, but find we cannot be independent of men, and that's

Introduction

a problem. What I learned from watching what my mother went through is fear and longing. Fear of and longing for motherhood, which I hold onto with my very teeth despite the taste. Fear of and longing for men—who I cannot avoid loving, who I emulate *and* desire. Longing for the joy of a dream come true. Fear of failure—inevitable. I am constantly filling in holes in myself by digging soil out of myself.

I want all that men are willingly given, but constantly wonder— do I then give up what it means to be a woman? By following my ambitions to success and to self-reliance do I forego the right to be loved by a man? Saddled by a disease like mine, must I work twice as hard to do either? Can I not have children because I'm ill, or because I must be successful because I'm ill? Perhaps all my aspirations have left no room for the "maternal instinct"— maybe I'm not even fit to have children. My mother felt she may not be a "good woman". I feel like I may not be a woman at all.

My question is that of self-made women. The answer is that independence is not a privilege but a human need. So is love and family. Until both sexes agree that we do not shed one to embrace the other, we'll be always asking, "What did I do wrong?" We'll hate

Spinning

each other for loving each other and chastise
ourselves for wanting what all humans want.

But our freedom is not the disease and guilt and fear
the symptoms—rather, guilt and fear are the
medication we keep force-feeding ourselves for having
what every human cannot live without. We're busy
curing ourselves of humanity. The cycle is the side
effect of the cure.

— *Ann Stewart*

A Third Eye. 2006

Poetry as intervention is a strong healing tool. How
poetry works its magic remains a mystery after years
of workshops, study and writing.

As nurses and teachers, Judy and I found common
ground in reading and writing poems. Our shared
interest in exploring the soothing and comforting
effects of poetry as self-care formed the basis of a
strong personal and professional friendship. Reading
the work of classic bards as well as more modern
poets and lyricists delighted us. We loved finding
and reading the works of favorites from Gibran,
Rilke, Rumi, Basho, May Sarton, Wendell Berry,
Marge Piercy, Shel Silverstein to name only a few.

Introduction

Judy's history with writing poetry created a space to express passions, griefs and the processing of life's events. Her work grew like her garden, with perennial themes thriving beside those seasonal annuals that bloom and move on. Her gentle and gracious heartwords touch and comfort.

My "poeming" history started with a desire for greeting cards that went beyond marketed sentiments. Word play and rhyme provided a container for sharing the emotions and fun of formal or casual family occasions. The haiku form became combined with my impressions from nature to help focus my observations of family, work and self, as life happened.

As Judy and I shared our common ground of nursing, we also reinforced our practice of personal poetry with each other, then with individual patients. Single-case methodology reinforced the power we saw when people used writing personal poetry to self-comfort, reassure, find therapeutic responses and make expanded sense of their experiences of health and illness. This is healing: making whole, mending or giving meaning.

Spinning

Personal poetry became an intervention we used as we encouraged self-health management with people in our nursing practices. Self-health management works to support people who adapt satisfactory solutions or reframed concepts of health. Writing and poetry became part of a repertoire of interventions that complemented traditional solutions to promote balance and respond to stressors. We've watched for many years and still stand in awe when someone gets an a-ha that helps move them toward new solutions or soothed pain. Not always achieving the ideal—but always striving toward understanding and self-management.

We also watched the regeneration of our love of poetry in our children. My offspring think poetry is silly, but it appears and is appreciated at family occasions and in times of stress.

In Judy's daughter, Annie, the seed grew as she faced her life's challenges. She polished her poetry skills to create a level of expression that can heal us all as we savor her images. Her poetry touches dark places in our souls and emerges on its way to wholeness and health. Whether personal and private or professionally cultivated and communal, poetry's

Introduction

power to heal has an impact that is palpable, if not concrete.

How does poetry work to heal? Damned if we know. Years of study and play with the connection between poetry, healing and communication have identified some possibilities for understanding its strength.

Writing poetry gives us a chance to look at something and see it differently, shift that perspective and give new meaning. It expands our insights, as we put it into a container of rhythm or seek a metaphor to make meaning. Sharing poetry lets others participate in our experience. The rhythm of patterns offers reassurance and common ground. One cannot deny the power of repeated nonsensical word rhymes and rhythms to settle restless, pre-language grandchildren and frazzled parents, grandparents. Capturing a moment for a group to craft a poetic mission statement creates collaboration that lasts.

Sharing poetry also validates our responses, while allowing us to expand our insights. It prevents festering and instead purges or cleanses to allow and foster development of awareness. Our self-efficacy is promoted through exploration of emotions and the possibilities of alternatives. These perspectives allow

Spinning

mindful participation in an evolution that includes satisfactions well beyond basic survival.

Poets and women have long included spinning in their work of daily living: spinning threads, stories, webs, connections and relationships. This collection of poems spun between mother and daughter offers a chance to feel the power of poetry as it spins its mystery and magic.

— *Barb Groh*

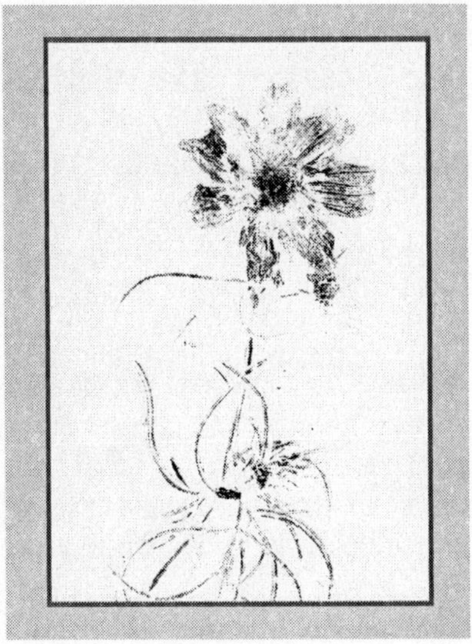

Spinning

Infection

Spinning...
Mother. Daughter. Each
in her own orbiting.
Crisscross. Connect.

Collide with dizzying energies
that hurt, help, inhibit,
infect.

Guilts. ghosts. gifts.
swirl in galaxy of
private poems and secret truths.

Daughter. Mother.
Spinning...

— *B. Groh, 2006*

Spinning

A Woman's Experience — Choices

I came along at a time when women
Knew what they had to do and did it.
Marriage, home and family.
Demure — Consider the overtures
But never extend them.
Build your cooking skills
and give yourself
to your children.
A good mother always stays home.

And then my mother changed the rules —
only slightly but gave me a glimpse
and I saw the possibilities and
felt the difference.
Permission with qualifiers,
I took the offer.
Not really understanding
The forces that would invade.
A yearning to do it all — succeed —
Guilt for not cooking

Infection

Dinner every night.
And I continue to struggle
This struggle continues —
Delicious at times,
But pulls in more directions
Than I can go.
Pondering the challenge of
Making a project work.
Wondering if staying home
Would have kept her well.
Enjoying the risk of overtures
And the resulting escape.
Puzzling the effects on a son's self image
When I am out building my own.
Wondering if they can really learn to be happy if I
Am not always there to orchestrate
Knowing that the choices made expand my world,
I answer the questions asked —
And then put the answers
On the witness stand.

— J. Stewart Hoelscher, 1985

Spinning

Baroness

I have a zillion stuffed animals jammed in cardboard
>boxes
Jammed into a cube like a car in a trash compactor.
I admit I want to take them out again—for myself.
Really—who wants
camel colored shit in the white of my French
>manicured nails.
To induce something hot and always sticky to vomit
over my shoulder—good hair takes *time*!
How I hate that sweet—not nicely sweet
but antifreeze sweet smell and
the rustle of diaper on fat little legs, sitting
on my Donna Karan New York pants
which by the way will *have* to be dry cleaned.
I prefer not to think of myself as a defunct appliance.
A faucet that spits only air and rust.
A radio which will play no jazz or R&B—
only twangy country or alternative crap.
Not a man but not a real woman either.

Infection

I think I am a sweater unworn, without a dot of lint or
>frayed armpit.
My uterus will forever be pink and smooth,
>unstretched
As the day I was born.
Therefore I refuse to sentence myself.
I don't deserve to do time in a dungeon of little pills.
Even though I dream of having dead babies,
their blue heads stuck in there like a cat in a chimney,
still in me and already decaying.
sometimes as I am about to sleep I see them
hideously misshapen—a mouth full of teeth making up
>the whole face,
I hear a low muffled cry from a hand grown into its
>cheek,
or a wormlike squirmer with no limbs and no face.
I blink it away and think hard
of Jacobson's shoe department and sales on at Lord
>and Taylor.

— *A. Stewart, 1996*

Spinning

Turn around

Every day I think about
the part of my life that breaks free
of routine work.
The message of perfection only.
Competition, crowding.
Turn off the radio and dance
Touch my plants
And watch the sun disappear or rise
Every day I
clear my desk, clear my mind and think
about turning it around.

— *J. Stewart Hoelscher*

Infection

Uninspired

What I feel right now is nothing.
I am not pinching back steamy
tears of sadness
or biting my lip in sweaty frustration.
I am not wallowing
in cold, muddy depression
or nursing resentful anger
with a therapeutic sulk and
lips thick with attitude.
I feel not the warmth and comfort
of being contented as I do in sleep.
My cheeks are not lit and
my heart is not tickled
with tasty, transient happiness.
no hyperactive jumpiness,
no hunger, no thirst.
My soul is as hollow today
as a discarded toilet paper roll.

—A. Stewart, 1994

A Woman's Experience — Exploration

I want to touch him —
A feeling so nice and strong
Tell me, is it just me?
Am I really different?
I guess I just need some reassurance
that feeling is o. k.
because it's such a restoring urge,
one I wouldn't trade
—And yet I am bound—
And what would happen if I did?
Or is it better not to feel?

— *J. Stewart Hoelscher*

Infection

Loneliness

sitting slumped.
my body has grown still like the furniture.
the silence's hum becomes a roar,
pounding, exploding in my brain.
this apartment seems abandoned.
even as I sit, lay, stand, sit in it again.
it has become like a hotel.
I'm just staying for a business trip.
even in the day the room seems dark.
the sunlight is like yellow blackness.
I can't tell when night comes.
happy voices, music, cars whizzing by.
sounds drift in windows.
mocking the empty drawer of my new life.
I am a ghost haunting myself.
— *A. Stewart, 1996*

Spinning

Escape

How can I tell you what
our relationship means
without incriminating me—
or frightening you with words
that get too close.
I so much like your gentle
warmth—a large part sensual
The way your skin feels
Hearing about your two-year old
The sounds that come when you do
Knowing you built a pool
The taste of your neck
Feeling a pride of success in physical exertion
Nipples tickled by chest hair
Telling stories of your early marriage

Infection

I wonder what it is that got you there
and what it is that keeps you sensitive
I wonder if we can be friends
With physical escape—
or without.

— J. Stewart Hoelscher

Spinning

Death By Hanging

Infatuation is a tightening noose
which first sits loosely
looped about my neck.
and its danger does not yet seem real—
Until the object of my desire finds me out
then the knot presses against
the nape of my neck and
my throat is constricted suddenly—
I am gasping for a way out when
rejection kicks the chair
out from beneath me
and I am left hanging suspended—
There I sway, rocking, struggling,
desperate for air but,
the rope keeps squeezing
as I slowly die choking and groaning.

— A. Stewart, 1994

Infection

Love

Struggling quiet, I
Hide a word
That crouches in the corner
Of my head,
Evades my tongue.
Too pale beside the feeling,
Margaret Atwood ringing,
"A word we use to plug holes
With...the right size for those
Blanks in speech."
Lying crumbled—
Credibility leaking out
A small hole in the side.
Bent on changing, I
Shake it out to use.
Wrap its shrinking
Form around a tongue to
Make it match the feeling,
Prop it up to push

Spinning

Away the walls that
Hide a part of being.
Margaret Atwood ringing,
"A finger grip on a cliffside.
You can hang on or let go."
— *J. Stewart Hoelscher, 4/83*

Infection

The Worm

There's a slimy worm
crawling in the pit of my throat
boring and chewing and,
squirming as it goes—
This worm known as
Jealousy, is a persistent thing
I can't seem to heave it forth
or be rid of it by swallowing—
The pain starts as a tickle but
this parasite eats me up like a leaf
and my flesh is torn and dismembered
when I am worm infested—
Soon my heart is bruised and
hole-filled like a rotten apple
and my worm-ridden eyes
fail to see clear.

— A. Stewart, 1994

Spinning

Expectations

While I knew
Better than to expect anything,
(What had I seen of its value?)
or maybe I didn't try it (recognize my need)
There was empty space; longing
That kept me looking
And then I jumped
Liquid sensation holding me up
He makes me smile, expecting love.

— *J. Stewart Hoelscher, 10/87*

Infection

Two Bites over the Edge

Singled handed (lipped)
You took me (us, actually)
Pissy, hot, bone tired.
Dealing in clogged suction tubes, no space
Adolescents wounded, acting out
Their lives by dancing on desks
Taking up sticks (like their fathers)
To fight back.
Single-handed (lipped)
You (playfully)
Suggested we could do anything.

— *J. Stewart Hoelscher, 5/93*

Electrode

The black box mapping
direction is
operated by
remote. My sense
and emotion switch
as controlled by
the power source: You.
By pulling a
lever: a piercing
phone receiver
slam, voice corrupted
into angry hiss.
By pressing the
red button: brown eyes
glaring beneath
ferocious brows. Blue
sparks stinging my
blood your hard scolding
is. A numbing

Infection

vibration of ev'ry
muscle is your
indifference. Your
nearness, like a
microphone too close
to the source makes
feedback. So fails the
mechanism:
signals disrupted,
wires helplessly
crossed up. Your eyes
so wide they speak like
open mouths. Your
voice touches—the skin
of a peach on
my eardrum. Your skin,
as carefully
as its warm hairy
surface brushes
me, I see that patch

Spinning

>as clearly as
>a heart-shaped tattoo.
>Electrodes. My
>temples picking up
>thick static like
>gamma rays burning
>cell after cell.
>
>— *A. Stewart, 1998*

Infection

A Child's Pain

She hurts and the feeling floods
Every joint I own
—Without wanting I go down—
With her—thinking that
At some time I'll change.
A suit of armor
Magic
Assistance from the gods
Reasoning

Because it doesn't seem
To be within my being
To shed that trip.

— *J. Stewart Hoelscher, 10/82*

The Offer

The day I first heard that you would
have it all your life—progressive—
I bargained with the gods.
I know that it's a cliché by now
but for the first time I understood
the meaning—and I couldn't stop myself.
I will trade—let me trade!
I can deal with it for me.
It's a selfish request really
—because it would be easier—
or
maybe some sacrifice would appease.
I'll give it up today—and take
celibacy, sobriety, poverty—selfish,
because it would be easier,
I shut the door of my office to make
the offer—knowing that I would not
find the answer there. That it will be
a day to day thing with no solution—

Infection

But I want the gods to know that
the offer is still open.

— *J. Stewart Hoelscher, 1983*

Spinning

Protection

I think I'm an average mother
and protecting comes with that.
You came from school one day
    saying that some child teased,
        "You walk funny, how come?"
          Hurt feelings quickly passed
    Wisdom sensing curiosity
  rather than rejection.
    But more will come
    from inside you or others.
    When media pressure overwhelms,
    and social values clearly spell
    Perfect bodies allowed only
    and you feel your blown up knees
    and crooked legs.
I would like to buy you protection, shelter.
Cotton padding or a high board fence
but know that this I cannot do
that protection weakens

Infection

      that protection comes from values
Varied, reaching deep inside
Willingness to share self—acceptance
Couched in gentleness and warmth
And these values I will help you build
....................While I fill out
an order for a suit of armor
and promise pain for anyone
who threatens.

                —J. Stewart Hoelscher, 12/82

Spinning

18

Where are my long legs and
> sculptured face?

At eighteen I am five-foot three not
> five-foot eight!

I am a sparrow—
> small, homely and chubby.
>> *—A. Stewart, 1994*

Infection

Awareness

In the supermarket a woman shops.
her flesh out populates her bones,
folding itself into piles like laundry,
imitating the comforts of food,
abdomen a series of doughy loaves,
backside an enormous ripe peach.
children point and laugh impishly.
an older man cringes
scanning her from head to foot.
others avoid her touch
as though it would defile them
or smear them with grease.
their taunting bounces off her bubbles of flesh
and smacks me sharply.
I want to be next to her,
walk beside her,
lay my head on her meaty shoulder,
shrink myself away.
we cross paths.

Spinning

I glimpse at her not meaning to.
I feel how spindly and branch-like I am.
but at home looking in the mirror
her penguin-y forms stares back,
weepy and out of breath.

— *A. Stewart, 1996*

Planning

A poem on Franklin Planner paper
has a certain air.
Born in a hurried day
Stark gray-like those
Wall Street suits, bustling from
One decision to another
No soft words here
Only gray reflected
in my eyes, skin.
Think about how that happens
Taken over by a planner-by one
serious problem that grows.
Crowding out quick laughter,
Lunch in the sun
A side trip through an antique shop
Time with friends.
Ceremony to burn is next in line.

— *J. Stewart Hoelscher*

Spinning

Air/Ground

Up here it seems easy
A clear Florida coastline
Maps
A pilot to take me
Where I need to be
Ground is different

Bumps
And barriers
Road construction
Detours
Make a journey a challenge.

— *J. Stewart Hoelscher*

Infection

75 South

    cow's ass, grickle grass
      tiny towns,   patches of brown
Oaks curse at me
behind electric fences
      screaming green nothing between
    traffic sighs   raccoon eyes

withering corn   barreling orange
    time's round   driving down
                I'll deal with

  losing you
when I get there.

                  — *A. Stewart, 2001*

Spinning

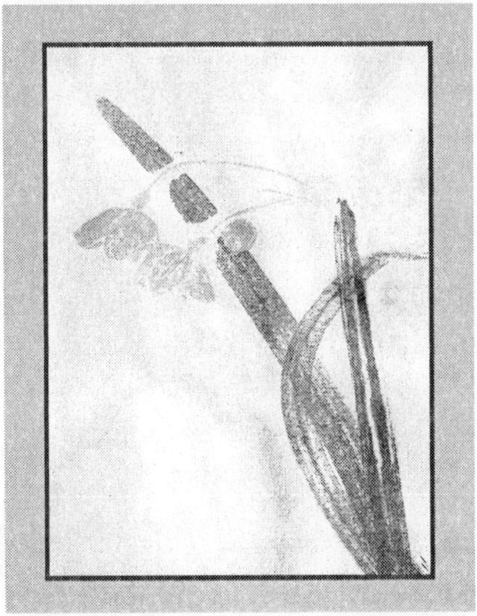

Spinning

Rehabilitation

Spinning...
Hard pedal and drive to
exorcize old devils
—the ones we know—

then cycle, re-cycle
before any real change.
And re-cycle, re-cycle
'til real change—to ones we don't know?

Mother. Daughter.
Spinning...

Webs. Shared patterns:
Prayers, poems, paths.
Recall, resolve, reward
Daughter. Mother.
Spinning...

— *B. Groh*

Spinning

Up and Down

I feel like I am in the middle
Being pulled by forces
I have chosen
Good and bad
I am in control
And I accomplish the deadlines
With a sense of success so important to me
Only to reinvest myself
In causes of concern
More forces
That pull me in directions
Entirely of my choosing experiencing pleasure
With pain that comes in any course chosen
And I continue to explore my alternatives
To decide if there are other ways;
Or are the ups and downs evidence of living?

—*J. Stewart Hoelscher 1982*

The Ballad of Little Pig and Farmer Joe

Little pig, little pig
Won't you come out of the mud today?
The sun is above you,
And ever I love you,
But there in the mud with my heart you lay.
Shall I offer you an orange rind?
A succulent coffee grind?
The skin from my knees?
The white of my teeth?
But to hear you grunt and bury your face
Deep in the filth and pugnacious decay?
Save me a sucking oozing slot,
For my sympathetic skin is hot.

Spinning

Kissing the worms, eating the shit.
Depression burns slow like a roasting pit.
Perhaps some bacon to flavor my bread;
Perhaps my own blood
On toast instead.
Little pig, little pig
Won't you come out of the mud?

— A. Stewart, 2000

Rehabilitation

A Woman's Experience — Risk

Woman's experience
has been demure.
The urge to make
overtures frightening.
The rejection lurking
would reduce, and
wanting is not good.
Passivity becomes comfortable—
The payoffs are there.
The confidence game
played seems to work.
Man alone can
take the risk
and survive—
Double standard!
that stifles risk,
and limits options!
Can our loss
be justified?

Spinning

And even when rejected,
aren't there gains?

— *J. Stewart Hoelscher*

Dream Ghosts

The baby on the velvet couch cries hard, her soft
    chest heaving.
She needs to be touched. She needs to be held.
Her chubby pale arms reach out to me.
Her stout legs extend to me urgently.
Suddenly she falls from the couch and I grab her
    desperately by one pristine, tiny foot.
Her screams awaken me and she disappears never to
    return.
The little girl is dressed in gauzy white.
She has been a good little girl.
She walks in a cold dark house polluted with dust,
    clutching a dolly, lips unpainted both.
She finds an icy gray bed and lies down between its
    rusty stained sheets, a moth caught in a wolf
    spider's web.
As she is dying, I cry into my pillow, then she is gone.

Spinning

The old woman appears in a living room without
    furniture, papery bent figure beneath a tuft of
    gray.
She is lying down, standing up.
She calls to me and I run from her whining voice, still
    in front of me. She disappears and yet she is
    there.
She will rise out of the cold bed.
She will slink forth from under the couch.
She is standing over me when I wake up, white
    daylight and black shadows creeping in.

                                          — *A. Stewart, 1997*

Rehabilitation

The Wall Building Myth

Once upon a time
In a nearby land
Lived fair maidens and fair gentlemen
In arrangements conducive
To the needs of both, or so it seemed.

For the fair maidens of the land
On every level and in every quarter
Knew and chose their part
And the fair gentlemen theirs
And they both lived together
In a harmony, or so it seemed.

The arrangement consisted of
The fair maidens being the
Childbearers, homemakers,
weavers of cloth, preparers of food—
The next generation came from their wombs.

Spinning

The gentleman took care
Of the maiden—brought
Home the money to purchase
The home—car, food and
Both depended on each other, or so it seemed.

And there came into the land
A strange maiden not so fair
Who suggested that there lurked
Below the surface of the arrangement
Potential for the fair maiden
To go out into the world—
Take care of the gentleman
By bringing home the money to
Purchase the home, car, food—
And a loud cry arose across the land!
For it seemed that this would be
Impossible considering the situation,
Which both fair maiden and gentleman
Knew to exist.

Rehabilitation

And that was, as everyone knew
And accepted, that the fair gentleman
Could deal with relationships
Of all kinds both male and
Female without jeopardizing
His responsible relationship to
Fair maiden at home.

While all knew that fair maiden
At home would fall in love; must morally
Fall in love in any relationship
With fair gentleman outside the
home.

And this frightened both, for
Both knew that once
Fair maiden ventured out into
The land, and developed relationships
With fair gentleman outside
The home the responsible

Spinning

Relationship to fair gentleman
At home would crumble.

Now the strange and not so fair maiden
Persevered—and it came to pass
That the fair maiden began to
Arrange (carefully so that all
Things at home were taken care
of) a way to venture out,
Reassuring the fair gentleman at
Home on every turn that she
Would take care of all and
That no other fair gentleman would
Enter her sphere. For she and he knew
That this would be disastrous
Considering her susceptibility to
Fall in love, and the potential of this
For destroying fair gentleman at home.

Rehabilitation

And one day it came to pass
that the fair maiden awoke
to the realization that she
had, in her ventures
Outside the home, met and dealt with
Many a fair gentleman in
A satisfactory way and it was pleasurable.
But she continued to hold them
At a distance knowing that
Any close relationship would result in love that
destroyed!
While the fair gentleman went
On his way doing what all
Fair gentlemen do; and they
Both knew and accepted this
As it had to be, or so it seemed.

Spinning

And walls went up around all the
fair maidens in the land—and the
Fair gentleman roamed the
Land at will, an arrangement
Conducive to meeting the needs of both
For they depended on each other, or so it
seemed.

Now the moral of the story
Might be twofold or three
So let us here discover
What that moral just might be

Is it that our fine, fair maiden
Should in the fair home stay
Keeping family together
Horrors—No, you say?

Rehabilitation

Or might it be fair gentleman
Out to change his own fair way
Limiting relationships to men
(A little humor—if I may!)

Or could it be that maidens
Fair and not so fair alike
Can develop relationships
With fair gentlemen all right.

And what of the myth of love
In relationships to be.
Will the maiden fall in love
And destroy her family?

It's herein, fair maiden sisters,
That the mystery surely lies
Should our love be defined?
Rationed—and just whose standards by?

Spinning

And just what is our love made of?
Are there one or many kinds?
And what shape does it come in?
Will we recognize the signs?

The questions must be answered
In another thousand years
But in the very near and meantime
The myth builds up the fears.

The questions that can be asked
And answered rapidly
Do fair gentlemen have more control
Or less mystic love capacity?

The answer is of course—not so!
Fair gentleman and maiden too
Must open up their lives to love
—to people, relationships, old and new.

Rehabilitation

Thus destroying this controlling myth
To rebuild in nearby land
A myth that h as no walls
But a "growing-love" demand.
— *J. Stewart Hoelscher*

Spinning

Marge Piercy to Me

#1
Some times I call
For my father's patience
When I rail-like Marge Piercy
"Charge in"
Knife-edge sharp
(protection is important)
Like a patient demanding
Good care.
Every nurse avoids that room
Genetic treasure gone
Knife-edge sharp
Only cuts you off

Rehabilitation

#2
What would it take?
To learn gentleness
Marge Piercy said it
That fear like a shock
Adrenalin builds a wall
And puts me between
Some robot like part of my
Head and heart, turns my body
Around and I walk away.

— *J. Stewart Hoelscher*

Spinning

Reentry

Takes some work
Move from a warm place.
Time callous
The light, sweet taste of knowing
No planners allowed
Move to wind chill and something pressing
Always that clenched
Body part
What did you get done today?
Echoes in my head.

— *J. Stewart Hoelscher*

Rehabilitation

The Dream

Night time is the worst time for a person living alone.
Last night I dreamt of a serial murderer.
He was a man balding, wisps of yellow hair flying
from the back end of his head.
He took tender, soft, rotting apricots between his
    thumb and fingers
and pulled them in two halves.
He used these as padding
for his thumbs as he gouged out the eyes of his
    victims.
Chanting perversely as he went,
walking two arms held out like a zombie.
I woke up blinking in the darkness, naked.
Though I was scorching in the dense heat
I pulled a sheet quickly over my body.
Though I was like a chicken spinning on a spit,
I shut and locked every window.
I examined each closet and room
for my apricot bearing attacker.

Spinning

I sweated on my pepper spray can in my bed, staring
 at the door.
The clicking of hangers was my locked being picked.
The humming of the fridge was my window sliding
 open.
I can see my ugly picture smiling on America's Most
 Wanted.
I'm unlucky enough to be the one out of four.
Trying to make shapes out of shadows,
I wait hours until the sun comes up.

— *A. Stewart, 1996*

Rehabilitation

I heard a phat break when I died
My mind follows a swirl
around my draining body
evacuating into a sewer
   of meaninglessness and
nonexistence.
Pulsations once thrummed through
this dust you run through your fingers.
   Gliding down the dark
green maelstrom
I thought I remembered
a heartbeat
but my memory was gone
in the air never to
be snagged again and thought was the
print of light in
air—a flash on a retina.

Spinning

A blinding warmth
—and blistering light
files itself
into the smooth-ebony grooves—
of my fledgling soul.

— *A. Stewart, 1998*

Rehabilitation

The Cycle

Intensity to care, and lofty goals
Cover for the
Mind—squared with projects
Gripped in Steel.
Three piece suits
And leather cases
Spew productivity in 60 hour weeks
Dark circles at the eyes
And muscles twitching.
With each success
Elation dwindles
The weight of
Expectation
Tears—
Survivors steal through
Convenient backdoors
Quietly finding distant places to
Feel downhill speed through powder
View scenes from Teton pass

Spinning

Drink Jack Daniels from the bottle
Touch the skin of mountain people
Until
The distant view
Lifts the weight
Of projects gripped in steel.
              — *J. Stewart Hoelscher, 4/83*

Rehab

The old snow forms cracks and rifts
   like veins in translucent hands
wounds bursting and prying apart
skin split by the sun
a twisted shrunken carcass
seeping into the earth
from the blood
The pointed snouts of earthworms
               make pores in the decay
   pulsing writhing stinking soil
   they chew the dirt, shit it out,
and eat it again
Come on, worm!
     wriggle and squirm
   from your cozy sludge
  be in motion
the crystal cage has faded and fled
   yielding to the searing sunlight

Spinning

Come up to cook your thin skin
and gnash your microscopic jaws
lash your slimy tail
   chew the dirt
    swallow it
    shit it out
    chew it
and swallow it again.

                   — *A. Stewart, 2000*

Rehabilitation

To Dr. S., from Annie's Mom

Dr. Silly started it
    When he sat her on his knee.
He said, "If they don't treat you right,
You can come to live with me.
We have malt and candy breakfasts,
Cake and ice cream for lunch,
Before squash, peas or spinach,
Eat all your sweets ... a must!
Well, she took it home to brother
Grinning—a game set to play,
and they went on forever
Giggling, laughing all the way.
There'll be no raking leaves
Until you've done your fishing,
And the T.V. must be watched
Or homework you'll be missing.
And on and on they went.
A million variations (and in the process)
Associating health care

Spinning

To laughter— celebration.
So, please add silliness to
That list of things you do,
Along with gentleness and warmth
That helps to get us through.
A lesson you would think I'd know,
But I have learned so much.
There's little pain that you can feel
When laughing, being silly, and such.
Thank you, kind man.
  — *Judy Stewart, October 21, 1982*

Check-up

White room. Sterile smell.
Glass jars. Yellowish diplomas.
Hollow nearing footsteps.
Beating heart. Sweaty brow.
Discomforting dread.

— *A. Stewart, 1994*

Sentence

If you've ever waited for hours
in a doctor's waiting room, then hours
on a cold examining table, or endured
watching your blood travel
in roller coaster spirals along
a tube to a vial from a needle
languishing inside the crook
of your arm, or heard
the condom/drugs lecture said
the same way in the same tone
for the umpteenth time, or received
a notice from a collection agency
demanding payment for that time
you were tortured, or learned
to automatically swallow something
supposedly good for you
that most noticeably just put you
to sleep or made you vomit,
or wondered if you would live to be

Rehabilitation

old while you waited endlessly
on the phone for that coveted
appointment two months away,
then you might understand why I choose
not to stay and listen to the old man
in his shiny tie and crisp slacks, staring
past me uninterested as he explains,
seated comfortably in his faux-
leather chair, physician's degrees gleaming
on the wall of his spacious office with a lovely
fountain view, that I must be
oh so careful, as a person
in my condition to read the fine print
on every policy as they do not
cover preexisting conditions, brushing
my pleas away smugly, because
after all, a person like me,
a statistical anomaly, loser of the genetic lottery,
a member of a community
of the sick, a sample, a seasoned

Spinning

> veteran in the health system
> of the United States,
> should know better.
> — *A. Stewart, 2000*

Trust I

Dropped like a ton of cold wet sand
or was it cement?
I hit that low
hearing you say
"I don't know what I want"
Those words still ring—and I hear
you say love
and wait for more wet sand (cement)

Trust II

One lone heron
Bruised wing
Watched beach people
pass
staying close
ready to fly
— *J. Stewart Hoelscher, 2006*

Enough

I planted flowers
Smiled
Cleaned every Saturday
Ironed
Listened to long
stories about education.
Licked your body and loved.
Something was not
enough.
What is enough to
keep your heart with mine?

—*J. Stewart Hoelscher, 2006*

Rehabilitation

South Haven Escape

Sitting still
In downtown South Haven
Shutting out
Those bad thoughts.
"What's wrong with me?"
"Such a shallow Asshole,"
"What did I do."
Lonely life.
And then look around and know.
I am lucky and can escape and go
listen to music
watch the men
laugh
healthy fun.

— J. Stewart Hoelscher, 2006

Spinning

Getting On I

Friends step in and I feel
that warm sun
at my back and
a powerful lifeline to getting on.

Getting On II

Learning to sit
Listen to songs sung—
birds know
what it takes—
One lone monarch butterfly
finds what it needs
in the bushes.
Lessons to learn.
Movement
Set free scared.
Time changed that as things
shut off opened.
Sisterhood gained

Rehabilitation

With each relationship/time spent.
Experiencing old love of things
set aside. Theatre, music,
kayak on peaceful water.
Marge Piercy-like
"Saving the only life I can."
— *J. Stewart Hoelscher, 2006*

Turtle Shell

Away
> from you I find myself trapped in a frozen pond,
> blind and deaf.

I smash my bony snout against the unforgiving ice.
A glimpse of you like sun is my breaking through.
I can breathe again.
> A flash of your shape, your balmy smell
> enwreathes me and then out of sight again.

Catching you at a phone, the curve of arm, the glint
> of hair and teeth.

The smile fondles my nerves and is
> gone again.

One day I will go looking and you will be gone for
> good.

Gasping, I will seek a jutting fleshy shoulder,
a freckled neck,
an eyelash.
But they won't be there or anywhere.

Rehabilitation

The ice will crack but permit only
    frozen darkness
    liquid ball bearings,
pushing me down to a tarry bottom as I
    swallow mud,
filling my lungs with freezing sludge.
They harden and I sink under leaden muck,
    sunless,
lightless chaotic void
sucking me out and flattening
me. going down
down deeper
                    deeper
forever
and ever
away.

                — *A. Stewart, 1998*

Spinning

Variation on the Subject

When you go, I will become the mummy,
Wrapped in a husk from head to toe, reeking
inwardly to myself.
My skull emptied by a hoop up my nose, juicily
dragging out my soul.
As your image is forgotten, my cells will become tiny
wrinkled kernels,
The memory of my love for you will be as Heaven.
I will ascend the pyramid gutless, brainless, gray
and dry.
There I will spend graceful eternity
In excess of nothingness.
Barren, rotting nicely
away.

—*A. Stewart, 1998*

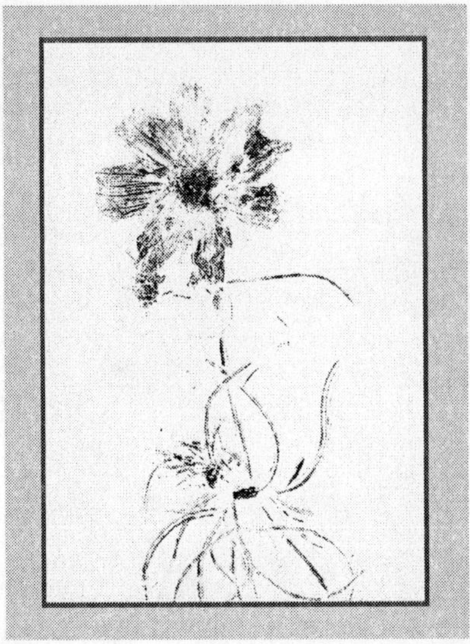

Spinning

Recovery

Spinning...

not cotton candy
but centrifuged sentiment to
sediment

Spinning...

to the core—
at the bottom of it
the meanings—the healings.

Spinning...
Mother, Daughter
gem poems

— *B. Groh, 2006*

Jungle Music

I once had a long languid dream
break from its gray, wet, and veiny membrane
and slide out a slit into hard cold consciousness.
In life it appeared a human
beautiful while still glistening in parts.
Small was my dream, quiet, not hardened all the way.
I punched his stomach once. It gelled
around my fist and snapped back again.
My hand was left coated with the smell of that sleep.
A warm white smell like soap on skin
and unwashed hair—my dream sculpted of flesh,
all my suffocated knowing wants, images
of my own heated creation,
slick night-dark hairs, childhood clouds breathing
    snow,
fast beats spun from scratching vinyl,
    my heaving dream
that imprisoned me in sweet sleep,
the jungle growing lurid about me,

Recovery

vines all encompassing cradling me in mid-air.
Then he flew far off and I fell.
Now my brain struggles, searching for my dream,
branches and vines digested by ice, snow buried,
my red fingers numb with digging.
The dream is forgotten; its steamy form
decaying away, seeping into wormy mud.
— *A. Stewart, 1998*

Spinning

Caring/Wanting

A gentle/man walks each day by
with will to make it better—takes the hand
and lifts what needs the care.
The measure given overflows
an empty place.
Giving he chooses—
A warm man and draws
me close by that.
The part that comes from
being near has left
a mark of want.
Our friendship kept but
little spent in building
The days go by
without an ease.
The gentle/man moves toward
an empty need, from healer work
And too much Caring.

Recovery

Helpless I watch to offer none
but a "come to me"—
Drawn by the wanting;
Hope to return the
friendship given.

— *J. Stewart Hoelscher, 5/83*

Spinning

Artificial Urgency

I love seeds
> My plants (friends) grow
> At a glance I know what they are
> Feel the dirt and feed.
> Mutual exchange I count on.
> Today I see some loss
> Brown fronds—too dry.
> Yellow leaves that lay on a cold window.
> Time passed (caught in the "urgent days)
> That mutual exchange is lost.
> Plants (friends) survive and I watch for my loss (brown fronds)
> Resolved to spend more time.
>> *— J. Stewart Hoelscher*

The New Leaf

For awhile I felt invisible.
I could forget the sound of my own voice.
When I heard it, it surprised me, like a bat
flying out of a dank cellar.
    I began to think I should get a cat
and rocking chair, and maybe a book of spells.
Frighten children for a living.
Stroking its fur and talking in its flea-bitten ears.
But without my invitation,
    I am now on someone's speed dial.
A co-shopper and crush-facilitator, now
employed by me.
It's like
just when I think my rubber plant
    will never sprout another new frond
    One tiny yellow spike
pushes through
  and uncurls.
What a relief it is.

                          — *A. Stewart, 1997*

Spinning

To Connie in Celebration of Knowing You Again

We had lost that special
Tasting of shared minds
Bonding to care
Knowing of mutual pain
While the business of our lives
Kept us away and culture instinct
To marry
To become—
    the "shoulds" and "musts"
Blurred that clear feeling
    of your life coming to mine.
    The chance of knowing again
has given me more than
can be said in words
found here or there

Recovery

I feel again
   That needed bonding
   That woman's telling and taking
that unconditional love that
you and I learn more of each day
I celebrate the renewal of our
   Friendship!

               — *J. Stewart Hoelscher, 6/83*

The Photograph

Three faces frozen in the past.
One wild night captured.
Hinting of wild times.
Unfamiliar now.
Three bright figures on night black.
Blonde heads, dangling earrings.
All a little bit drunk and
all different now.
Three people I haven't seen in months.
Except in a picture that
brings laughter ever so briefly.
Then I feel old.
Three bodies like mannequins.
Lips closed around a bottle.
Hands touching. Giggling.
Like a beer ad.
Three who were once buddies now
gone separate ways.
But still together in a picture.

— *A. Stewart, 1994*

Recovery

JOURNEY STORIES:
We Connect With Friends

3 Old broads meet again
Years of taking on what comes.
A magnet, our friendship
Draws and we give stories to
Each other—our lives.
Sharing soup, hearth, heart.
We are lucky, three old broads.

To Barb and Jackie 4-25-94
Where were we
Last Thursday?
3 old broads
Heads and hearts filled more
than most. Humor
struggling
In the heavy air.
Just because
we have credits,

Spinning

Because we know who's there
to give—we laugh and part OK.
How many students/patient's lives
Entered—Kids touched, raised
husbands, partner parted/joined?
Religion, feelings
Learning so much.
Tracking through heads and hearts
Three old broads—friends.
Who survive.
Where were we?
Three old broads
Reconnect, celebrate
Our lives, heart
Crossing.
We smile together...
Knowing.

Recovery

Who we are surpasses A+
For 3 old (teacher) broads.
How many ties
we have.

People, paths
Passion to keep it well
Plants—Poetry of our lives
— *J. Stewart Hoelcher*

Spinning

DED

My soul's residence is a cathedral of stalagmites
Yours is an aged deciduous forest.
Look upon it without eyes
Breathe without the bombardment of particles

In a corridor as deep as a mirror
And possessing a blinding darkness
Should I find the end of that cave
I will not walk toward the light
I will become the water that molds the subterranean
    rock
Should a house appear beneath the canopy, do not
    go in
You can try but you will not open that door
You have no hand with which to turn that knob
— *A. Stewart, 2000*

Recovery

Exercising

Warm, waves of pleasure
rush through every cell
thistledown sensations
against muscled surface
skin of gourmet worth
exhilarating exertion—
In spite of firm resolution
to hold distant
all the warm sensations
addiction comes.

From images
    that give caring
laughter
    that cannot be replaced
gentleness
that dictates every move
giving cause to reach for more and more.

— J. Stewart Hoelscher

Spinning

kisses

Your lashes jump like tiny unicorns
in glass domes kissing me with lips as soft
and dry as cotton. Guiltless, I want more:
a wetter touch and hotter weather. Wafts
of hair shampooed provokes a smile but make
me think of prairie grass bowing low
before a fire. Your beauty winds and quakes
like red-hued buds mid-freeze. We love for now
in careless light vibrations screened in bliss.
New leaves unroll as we walk by. We wait
like kids at Christmas: greedy for its gifts,
unblemished, God-like, royal, pure, and great.
So sugar sweet is happy love's pretense.
Such acrid burning is the consequence.

— *A. Stewart, 1998*

Recovery

Skiddish Part I 1-3-05

Sun always works
I stay in a safe spot (travel Daytona)
Ready to run
Vowing to do that
With the next doubt.
Who would think?
Work is comfort and I watch
His every move
Sure of another
Chapter to unfold.

Spinning

Skiddish Part II

It seems easy to stay
Here in Daytona and
No distraction.
(OK can I monitor his email, phone calls)
Passion—OK, company.
Nice skin
Humor
Staying still
Life with this man.

Skiddish Part III

"if you want certainty in your life, walk in darkness."
—*John Cross*

I take heart
Reassure.
Chaos and Calm—together
Friends, alone, shadow
All stay close

— *J. Stewart Hoelscher*

Recovery

Winter Branches

From crusted winter branches anger wakes,
Cold and silky coating like embalmment
In empty frozen veins that hatred leaks,
Seeping out a drippy sticky comment.
When sun or warming wind the flow dilute,
Trees spread their branches upward in the sky.
The stiff and icy hardness then be mute,
Storms and currents in a swishy decline,
Northern swirl that mixes and churns away.
I hope the leaves grow wide and block the sun.
I've learned to love the slimy dark decay
That cradles womb-like shrouds me all alone.
Just when I meet a chilly breeze like you,
I will prepare my winter branches new.
— *A. Stewart, 1996*

Spinning

Look Now At The Castle As It Stands

Features of the shore reshaped.
She smiles now through the day
And runs at water's edge, a stiff,
Slow, splash. Talking to a friend
Who comes out of her head.
Yesterday was only watching.
Without keeping to the now
I look between the railings
That divide my view, and
Line her up with what I see
Waiting for it all to change.
Some open gate lets in
The fear that lies ahead.
A call to come; a smile, that
Begs a closer look, take me
To a castle made of sand.
A pail of spinach waterweed is
Dinner, I am told. Two beetles—
Innocent passersby, are ushered

Recovery

To the supper party.
She brings me to a settled now
And shows me what I cannot do.
To think of pain that surely
Is a part of days to come
Is not this child's way.
Instead she brings me by to say
"Look Mom, at the castle as it
   stands."
                 — J. Stewart, April 1983

Before and After

In the evening,
moist air
ripe-smelling
like a cut open pear.
guttural, rumbling sounds,
trees whip to and fro
as if trying to uproot
and run.
avalanche of
smoke-gray clouds
rolls in like
thick, poisonous fumes.
purply gray sky
settles into dense blackness,
then vibrating low bass
becomes stampede of horses.
lightning briskly
makes night
like day accompanying

Recovery

explosions of thunder
like a giant balloon
popping...
In the morning,
serene quiet
fresh, muddy scent
fills the warm
rain-cleansed air
which dries shiny
soaked tree trunks
and newly emerald grass.
Sun twinkles through branches
reflecting off
raindrops like mirrors
clinging to the
shimmering wet leaves.
— *A. Stewart, 1994*

Spinning

Annie Now

Skipping softly
Kneeling to pet
A small black dog
Whose enthusiasm
Once irritated
Now brings a smile
Nose thoroughly licked
A chase starts
Cause to rejoice!

— J. Stewart, 1/28/83

Recovery

About Annie

It started when she was three years old—
a baby—with one innocent large finger—
At five her struggle to walk and run
leaves a pain in my throat and chest.
What is to be come of her—or me?
    At 40 years my values lie
    in shallow areas—granted,
    but shape my concern—
    the attention given long,
    thin legs has fed my ego—
    heads turn—
I watch her and muse,
A self-taught reader teaching her
teddy bear to read—for hours.
listening to "Free to be You and Me" and
knowing the message.
Drawing insects and wild flowers authentic—
with labels.

Spinning

Puzzling brother–sister relationships
with wisdom beyond her years.
Shaping her values
And the realization comes that she is, at seven years,
stronger and far ahead, with values that will hold
her through—realization, with relief and my
shoulders straighten—we go outside and play and run.
And the pain creeps back into my throat and chest.
— J. Stewart Hoelscher, 1983

Recovery

Grandpa Hoenes

I look back at him—earth courted.
In early dawn he did what he had done
each day past. Hoe in hand, cornmeal
breakfast solid in his middle, he went to
the garden that grew up around him—
set his life. I see him squeeze a hand filled
with dirt, mumbling.
"We sure do need some rain."
The essence of his getting through was
simple value; treat it gently, hope
for a good crop— a quiet smile.
Each spring pulled him with a
force that only plowing seemed
to still. He could will
the seed beyond the usual growing.
We never went home empty handed.
A simple life that grew a peaceful,
easy changing. Watermelon seed
spitting contests—silly laughing

Spinning

taught us what was first.
He took us as we were—the things we
Brought to him were always best.
We came and went and
each time gained without
a knowledge of it.
His autumn season came too quickly
I think about confused and solitary days
that took away his usual way of going.
Left him with an empty bent knee
smile...A mindless busy wandering
clearly showed our losses.
Never conscious of his giving—
We missed the man.
And now—I watch my father,
his son, my son—the lives
that come to me. And realize
that simple values come along with
peaceful, easy changing—the taking
as it is follows down the line.

Recovery

I know his meaning will be with us
And feel better for my son
to know the man stays near.
> — *J. Stewart Hoelscher, 5/83*

Spinning

To Grandpa

You once built us a mansion
with hay covered floors
and cobweb chandeliers
and many sawdust-smelling rooms
the kittens and horses were our children.
You once dug us up an Amazon
with drooping willow vines
the frogs and crayfish were alligators
and I, the jungle explorer
would dive deep into its silty dark.
You once grew us a daily feast
like the Pilgrims we savored
the sweet golden, crunchy green,
tart crimson, juicy fat red,
treats: all your humble gifts.

Recovery

So why can I only remember
your disillusionment and pain,
your panic and confusion,
your shakings and mumblings,
I curse the disease which robbed us of your memory.
— A. Stewart, 1994

Spinning...

Mother. Daughter.
Gem poems.
Touchstones for the rest of us as we all

Continue...

...Spinning...

—B. Groh, 2006

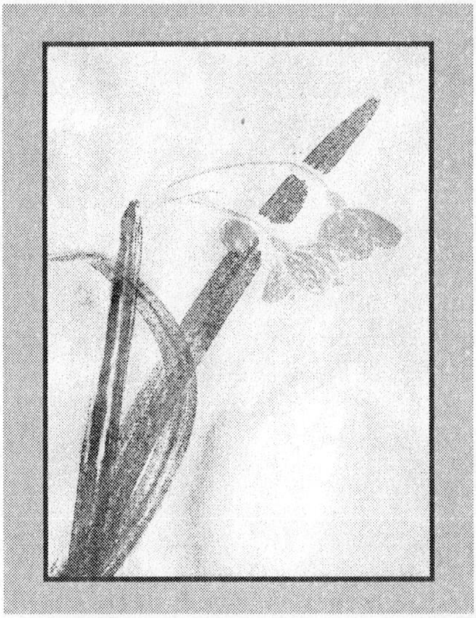

Spinning

Acknowledgements

Postscript from a Mom: June 2, 2006

Where to begin and what can I really say to capture how this journey had unfolded. My sincere thanks to the Bronson Auxiliary for their support to facilitate our ability to share our experience in the hope of offering something for healing.

For caring friends and an amazing daughter all who have changed my life. What I have learned! Not unlike MasterCard—Priceless! (Humor has been an important part.)

My thanks to Jackie Wylie and Barb Groh for their support and wisdom/talent—for friendship beyond words to describe. But let me try. I will be grateful through life for these people…

Postscript from Ann: June 2, 2006

For their kind and generous support I would like to give my thanks and love to Barb Groh and Jackie

Spinning

Wylie, and my appreciation to Barb, Diane Worden and Holley Lantz for cover design and technical help. Marge Wolf, a Kalamazoo artist, provided the line drawing of the authors. Most of all, I thank my mother Judy—she continues to be an inspiration to me both as a successful woman and brilliant writer.

Resources

Arthritis

Arthritis Foundation
www.arthritis.org/communities/juvenile_arthritis/
 children_young_adults.asp

Arthritis Foundation
1330 West Peachtree St., NW
Suite 100
Atlanta, Georgia, 30309

Reading and Writing

Atwood, M. 1978. *Two headed poems.* New York: NY: Simon & Schuster.

Blyth, R.H. 1949. *Senryu: Japanese satirical verses.* Tokyo, Japan: Hokuseido.

Berry, W. 1964. *The country of marriage.* San Diego, CA: Harcourt Brace Jovanovich /HBJ. One volume of many favorites.

Elbow, P. 1989. *Embracing contraries.* Oxford, England: Oxford University Press. As well as others.

Gibran, K. 1952. *The prophet.* New York, NY: Alfred A. Knopf.

Langer, E. 1992. *Mindfulness.* Menlo Park, CA: Addison-Wesley.

Pennebaker, J. 1997. *Opening up: The healing power of expressing emotion.* New York, NY: Guiliford.

Piercy, M. 1987. *Early ripening.* New York, NY: Pandora.

Sewell, M., ed. 1991. *Cries of the spirit.: Celebration of womens spirituality.* Boston, MA: Beacon.

Silverstein S. 1979. *Light in the attic.* New York, NY: Harper Row. Among many.

Rico, G. 1983. *Writing the natural way: Using right brain techniques to release your expressive powers.* New York, NY: Tarcher.

Whyte, D. 1994. *The heart aroused.* New York, NY: Doubleday.

About the Authors

Judy Stewart Hoelscher has spent forty-two years in health care. Her commitment and beliefs center around caring and alternative ways of staying healthy. (And, along with that, she has worked closely with physicians and nurses who provide medical and nursing care that heals. She has developed a healthy respect and admiration for the medical and nursing staff who have touched her daughter, Ann's life and her own.) Writing is one healing way that has been a mainstay for Judy, reaching out to understand the best way to be a good mom and to deal with what life gives. Writing has been vital to help her stay focused on what is important...caring...and to know how lucky she is to have a wonderful daughter and friends who contribute significantly to her healing and to Ann's.

Ann Stewart was born in 1975 and raised in rural Allegan, Michigan. Diagnosed with Juvenile Rheumatoid Arthritis at age five, writing became a way for Ann to express that which her body could

Spinning

not. With her mother, she later moved to downtown Battle Creek and graduated from high school in 1994. She received a degree in English from the University of Michigan and obtained a master's degree in creative writing from Miami University of Ohio. After two years as an editor for an Ann Arbor publication, Ann enrolled in the University of Wisconsin at Milwaukee to obtain her doctorate and pursue a career teaching young people to write.

To order more copies of
SPINNING: Poems Spun between Mother and Daughter
by Ann Stewart with Judy Stewart Hoelscher

Each softcover copy is $12.95 with 40% for 10 or more copies.

copies _____ x _____ = $ _____

Shipping and Handling:
$3.00 for first book and
$1.50 for each additional book. $ _____

Tax: Michigan residents, add 6% sales tax $ _____

Checks payable to:
Alumni Association of BMH School of Nursing

Mail order form and payment to:
Alumni Association of BMH School of Nursing
c/o PO Box 20058
Portage, MI 49019

Send book/s to (please print):

Name _____

Street _____

City_____

State /Province _____ Zip _____